# BROWNING

Compiled and Illustrated by Patricia Machin

**Salem House Publishers**
Topsfield, Massachusetts

First published in the United States by Salem House Publishers, 1987
462 Boston Street, Topsfield, MA 01983

**Library of Congress Cataloging in-Publication Data**
Browning, Robert, 1812-1889.
  Browning.
  I. Machin, Patricia, 1920-    . II. Title.
  PR4203.M3   1987   821'.8   87-9532

ISBN 0-88162-300-8

First published in Great Britain 1985 by
Webb & Bower (Publishers) Limited
9 Colleton Crescent, Exeter, Devon EX2 4BY

Copyright © 1985 Webb & Bower (Publishers) Limited

All rights reserved. No part of this publication may be reproduced, stored in a retrieval system, or transmitted, in any form or by any means, electronic, mechanical, photocopying, recording or otherwise, without the prior permission of the copyright holder.

Typeset in Great Britain by P&M Typesetting Limited, Exeter, Devon

Printed and bound in Hong Kong by Mandarin Offset International Limited

## Contents

| | |
|---|---|
| Introduction | 4 |
| Pippa Passes | 6-9 |
| May and Death | 10 |
| My Last Duchess | 12-15 |
| Meeting at Night | 16 |
| One Way of Love | 18 |
| The Patriot | 20 |
| Saul | 22-25 |
| De Gustibus | 26-29 |
| Home Thoughts from Abroad | 30 |
| The Last Ride | 32-35 |
| Two in the Campagna | 36-39 |
| Childe Roland | 40-45 |
| Prospice | 46 |

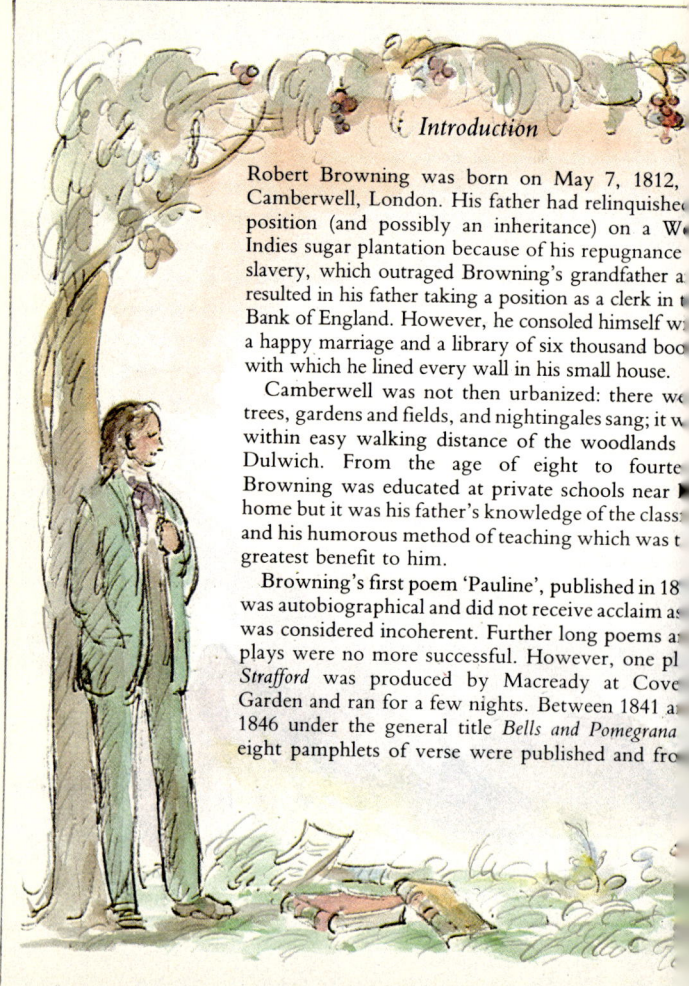

## Introduction

Robert Browning was born on May 7, 1812, Camberwell, London. His father had relinquished position (and possibly an inheritance) on a W Indies sugar plantation because of his repugnance slavery, which outraged Browning's grandfather a resulted in his father taking a position as a clerk in Bank of England. However, he consoled himself w a happy marriage and a library of six thousand boo with which he lined every wall in his small house.

Camberwell was not then urbanized: there we trees, gardens and fields, and nightingales sang; it w within easy walking distance of the woodlands Dulwich. From the age of eight to fourte Browning was educated at private schools near home but it was his father's knowledge of the class: and his humorous method of teaching which was t greatest benefit to him.

Browning's first poem 'Pauline', published in 18 was autobiographical and did not receive acclaim a: was considered incoherent. Further long poems a plays were no more successful. However, one pl *Strafford* was produced by Macready at Cove Garden and ran for a few nights. Between 1841 a 1846 under the general title *Bells and Pomegrana* eight pamphlets of verse were published and fro

this time the poet was accepted in literary circles.

The romantic story of Browning's love for the poet Elizabeth Barrett is very well known. Their letters to each other during the year he was visiting the invalid Elizabeth at her home in Wimpole Street and persuading her to leave her tyrannical father and elope to Italy with him were published after his death in 1899. On September 12, 1845, they were married secretly and a few days later made the hazardous journey to Italy where Elizabeth recovered her health and lived for another sixteen years. Their life together is a fascinating study and there are many records and letters for those who wish to know more about them and the times in which they lived. Elizabeth's father never forgave her, refusing to open the letters she sent. She never saw him again.

On Elizabeth's death, Browning returned to England with their son, Pen, aged twelve, and lived the rest of his life in a house overlooking the picturesque Regent's Canal in an area of London known as Little Venice. His output of poems increased as did his popularity. In America he had been popular for many years; Elizabeth had written to her sister in 1860: 'In America he is a power, a writer, a poet. He is read, he lives in the hearts of the people.' Browning died in Venice on December 12, 1889, and was buried in Westminster Abbey.

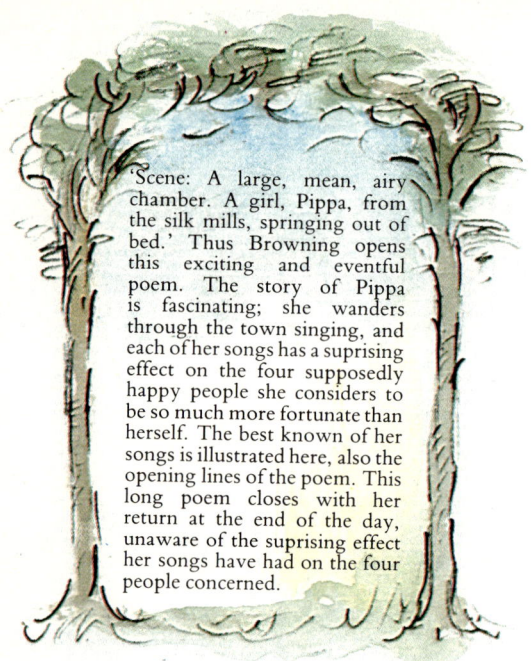

'Scene: A large, mean, airy chamber. A girl, Pippa, from the silk mills, springing out of bed.' Thus Browning opens this exciting and eventful poem. The story of Pippa is fascinating; she wanders through the town singing, and each of her songs has a suprising effect on the four supposedly happy people she considers to be so much more fortunate than herself. The best known of her songs is illustrated here, also the opening lines of the poem. This long poem closes with her return at the end of the day, unaware of the suprising effect her songs have had on the four people concerned.

*Pippa's Song*

The year's at the spring
And day's at the morn;
Morning's at seven;
The hill-side's dew-pearled;
The lark's on the wing;
The snail's on the thorn:
God's in his heaven—
All's right with the world!

## *Pippa Passes*

Day!
Faster and more fast,
O'er night's brim, day boils at last:
Boils, pure gold, o'er the cloud-cup's brim
Where spurting and suppressed it lay,
For not a froth-flake touched the rim
Of yonder gap in the solid gray
Of the eastern cloud, an hour away;
But forth one wavelet, then another, curled,
Till the whole sunrise, not to be suppressed,
Rose, reddened, and its seething breast
Flickered in bounds, grew gold, then overflowed the
world.

Oh, Day, if I squander a wavelet of thee,
A mite of my twelve hours' treasure,
The least of thy gazes or glances,
(Be they grants thou art bound to or gifts above
measure)
One of thy choices or one of thy chances,
(Be they tasks God imposed thee or freaks at thy
pleasure)
—My Day, if I squander such labour or leisure,
Then shame fall on Asolo, mischief on me!

Thy long blue solemn hours serenely flowing,
Whence earth, we feel, gets steady help and good—
Thy fitful sunshine-minutes, coming, going,
As if earth turned from work in gamesome mood—
All shall be mine! But thou must treat me not
As prosperous ones are treated, those who live
At hand here, and enjoy the higher lot,
In readiness to take what thou wilt give,
And free to let alone what thou refusest;
For, Day, my holiday, if thou ill-usest
Me, who am only Pippa,—old-year's sorrow,
Cast off last night, will come again to-morrow:
Whereas, if thou prove gentle, I shall borrow
Sufficient strength of thee for new-year's sorrow.
All other men and women that this earth
Belongs to, who all days alike possess,
Make general plenty cure particular dearth,
Get more joy one way, if another, less:
Thou art my single day, God lends to leaven
What were all earth else, with a feel of heaven, –
Sole light that helps me through the year, thy sun's!

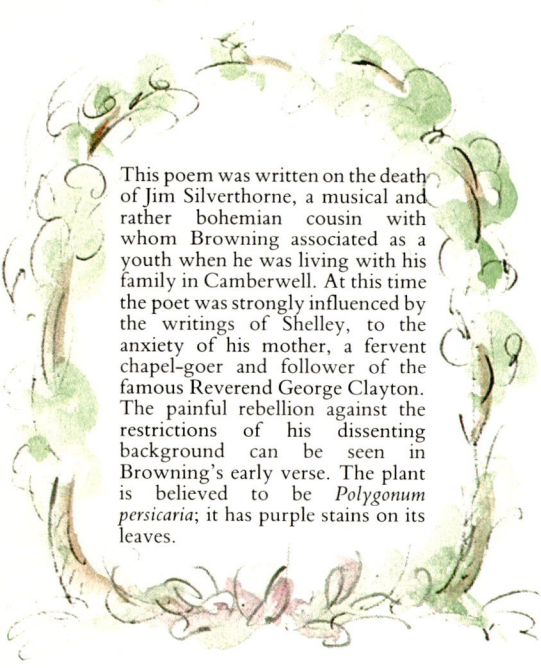

This poem was written on the death of Jim Silverthorne, a musical and rather bohemian cousin with whom Browning associated as a youth when he was living with his family in Camberwell. At this time the poet was strongly influenced by the writings of Shelley, to the anxiety of his mother, a fervent chapel-goer and follower of the famous Reverend George Clayton. The painful rebellion against the restrictions of his dissenting background can be seen in Browning's early verse. The plant is believed to be *Polygonum persicaria*; it has purple stains on its leaves.

## *May and Death*

I wish that when you died last May,
   Charles, there had died along with you
Three parts of spring's delightful things;
   Ay, and, for me, the fourth part too.

A foolish thought, and worse, perhaps!
   There must be many a pair of friends
Who, arm in arm, deserve the warm
   Moon-births and the long evening-ends.

So, for their sake, be May still May!
   Let their new time, as mine of old,
Do all it did for me: I bid
   Sweet sights and sounds throng manifold.

Only, one little sight, one plant,
   Woods have in May, that starts up green
Save a sole streak which, so to speak,
   Is spring's blood, spilt its leaves between,—

That, they might spare; a certain wood
   Might miss the plant; their loss were small:
But I,—whene'er the leaf grows there,
   Its drop comes from my heart, that's all.

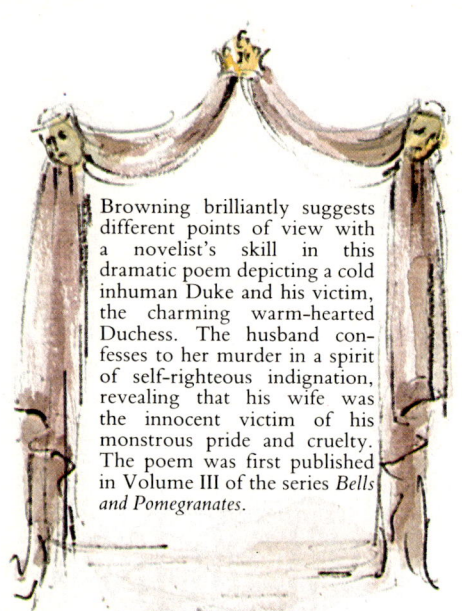

Browning brilliantly suggests different points of view with a novelist's skill in this dramatic poem depicting a cold inhuman Duke and his victim, the charming warm-hearted Duchess. The husband confesses to her murder in a spirit of self-righteous indignation, revealing that his wife was the innocent victim of his monstrous pride and cruelty. The poem was first published in Volume III of the series *Bells and Pomegranates*.

## *My Last Duchess*

THAT'S my last Duchess painted on the wall,
Looking as if she were alive, I call
That piece a wonder, now: Fràa Pandolf's hands
Worked busily a day, and there she stands.
Will't please you sit and look at her? I said
'Fràa Pandolf' by design, for never read
Strangers like you that pictured countenance,
The depth and passion of its earnest glance,
But to myself they turned (since none puts by
The curtain I have drawn for you, but I)
And seemed as they would ask me, if they durst,
How such a glance came there; so, not the first
Are you to turn and ask thus. Sir, 't was not
Her husband's presence only, called that spot
Of joy into the Duchess' cheek: perhaps
Fràa Pandolf chanced to say 'Her mantle laps
'Over my lady's wrist too much,' or 'Paint
'Must never hope to reproduce the faint
'Half-flush that dies along her throat:' such stuff
Was courtesy, she thought, and cause enough
For calling up that spot of joy.

                              She had
A heart—how shall I say?—too soon made glad,
Too easily impressed; she liked whate'er
She looked on, and her looks went everywhere.
Sir, 't was all one! My favour at her breast,
The dropping of the daylight in the West,
The bough of cherries some officious fool
Broke in the orchard for her, the white mule
She rode with round the terrace—all and each
Would draw from her alike the approving speech,
Or blush, at least. She thanked men,—good! but thanked
Somehow—I know not how—as if she ranked
My gift of a nine-hundred-years-old name
With anybody's gift. Who'd stoop to blame
This sort of trifling? Even had you skill
In speech—(which I have not)—to make your will
Quite clear to such an one, and say, 'Just this
'Or that in you disgusts me; here you miss,

'Or there exceed the mark'—and if she let
Herself be lessoned so, nor plainly set
Her wits to yours, forsooth, and made excuse,
—E'en then would be some stooping; and I choose
Never to stoop. Oh sir, she smiled, no doubt,
Whene'er I passed her; but who passed without
Much the same smile? This grew; I gave commands;
Then all smiles stopped together. There she stands
As if alive. Will't please you rise? We'll meet
The company below, then. I repeat,
The Count your master's known munificence
Is ample warrant that no just pretence
Of mine for dowry will be disallowed;
Though his fair daughter's self, as I avowed
At starting, is my object. Nay, we'll go
Together down, sir. Notice Neptune, though,
Taming a sea-horse, thought a rarity,
Which Claus of Innsbruck cast in bronze for me!

This romantic little poem was first published in 1845 in Volume VII of *Bells and Pomegranates*. This was a memorable year for the poet; in September he secretly married Elizabeth Barrett and left England with her to settle first in Pisa and then in Florence. He had already visited Italy twice: in 1838 in search of material for his autobiographical poem 'Sordello' and again in 1844.

## Meeting At Night

The grey sea and the long black land;
And the yellow half-moon large and low;
And the startled little waves that leap
In fiery ringlets from their sleep,
As I gain the cove with pushing prow,
And quench its speed i' the slushy sand.

Then a mile of warm sea-scented beach;
Three fields to cross till a farm appears;
A tap at the pane, the quick sharp scratch
And blue spurt of a lighted match,
And a voice less loud, thro' its joys and fears,
Than the two hearts beating each to each!

'One Way of Love' and 'The Patriot' were both published in the volume *Men and Women* in 1855. It is believed that Browning took the idea for 'The Patriot' from the old story of Arnold of Brescia, who vigorously condemned the power of the clergy and papacy and started the revolution that brought about the Roman Republic in 1155, but was siezed and executed by order of the Pope.

## One Way of Love

ALL June I bound the rose in sheaves.
Now, rose by rose, I strip the leaves
And strew them where Pauline may pass.
She will not turn aside? Alas!
Let them lie. Suppose they die?
The chance was they might take her eye.

How many a month I strove to suit
These stubborn fingers to the lute!
To-day I venture all I know.
She will not hear my music? So!
Break the string; fold music's wing:
Suppose Pauline had bade me sing!

My whole life long I learned to love.
This hour my utmost art I prove
And speak my passion—heaven or hell?
She will not give me heaven? 'T is well!
Lose who may—I still can say,
Those who win heaven, blest are they!

## *The Patriot*

### An Old Story

It was roses, roses, all the way,
   With myrtle mixed in my path like mad:
The house-roofs seemed to heave and sway,
   The church-spires flamed, such flags they had,
A year ago on this very day.

The air broke into a mist with bells,
   The old walls rocked with the crowd and cries.
Had I said, 'Good folk, mere noise repels—
   'But give me your sun from yonder skies!'
They had answered, 'And afterward, what else?'

Alack, it was I who leaped at the sun
   To give it my loving friends to keep!
Nought man could do, have I left undone:
   And you see my harvest, what I reap
This very day, now a year is run.

There's nobody on the house-tops now—
   Just a palsied few at the windows set;
For the best of the sight is, all allow,
   At the Shambles' Gate—or, better yet,
By the very scaffold's foot, I trow.

I go in the rain, and, more than needs,
   A rope cuts both my wrists behind;
And I think, by the feel, my forehead bleeds,
   For they fling, whoever has a mind,
Stones at me for my year's misdeeds.

Thus I entered, and thus I go!
   In triumphs, people have dropped down dead.
'Paid by the world, what dost thou owe
   'Me?'—God might question; now instead,
'T is God shall repay: I am safer so.

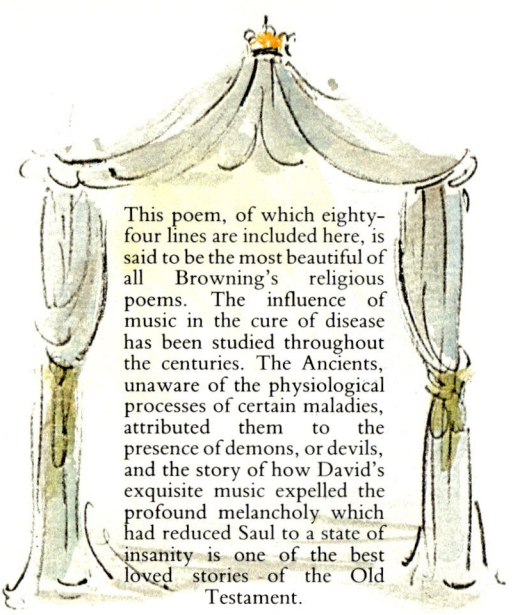

This poem, of which eighty-four lines are included here, is said to be the most beautiful of all Browning's religious poems. The influence of music in the cure of disease has been studied throughout the centuries. The Ancients, unaware of the physiological processes of certain maladies, attributed them to the presence of demons, or devils, and the story of how David's exquisite music expelled the profound melancholy which had reduced Saul to a state of insanity is one of the best loved stories of the Old Testament.

## Lines from Saul

Then I, as was meet,
Knelt down to the God of my fathers,
　And rose on my feet,
And ran o'er the sand burnt to powder.
　The tent was unlooped;
I pulled up the spear that obstructed,
　And under I stooped;
Hands and knees o'er the slippery grass-patch—
　All withered and gone—
That leads to the second enclosure,
　I groped my way on,
Till I felt where the foldskirts fly open;
　Then once more I prayed,
And opened the foldskirts and entered,
　And was not afraid;
And spoke, 'Here is David, thy servant!'
　And no voice replied;
And first I saw nought but the blackness;
　But soon I descried
A something more black than the blackness
　—The vast, the upright
Main-prop which sustains the pavilion,—
　And slow into sight
Grew a figure, gigantic, against it,
　And blackest of all;—
Then a sunbeam, that burst thro' the tent-roof,
　Showed Saul.

Then I tuned my harp,—took off the lilies
   We twine round its chords
Lest they snap 'neath the stress of the noontide
   —Those sunbeams like swords!
And I first played the tune all our sheep know,
   As, one after one,
So docile they come to the pen-door
   Till folding be done
—They are white and untorn by the bushes
   For lo, they have fed
Where the long grasses stifle the water
   Within the stream's bed;
How one after one seeks its lodging,
   As star follows star
Into eve and the blue far above us,
   —So blue and so far!

Then the tune for which quails on the cornland
   Will leave each his mate
To follow the player; then, what makes
   The crickets elate
Till for boldness they fight one another:
   And then, what has weight
To set the quick jerboa a-musing
   Outside his sand house
—There are none such as he for a wonder—
   Half bird and half mouse!
—God made all the creatures and gave them
   Our love and our fear,
To show, we and they are his children,
   One family here.

Then I played the help-tune of our Reapers,
   Their wine-song, when hand
Grasps hand, eye lights eye in good friendship,
   And great hearts expand,
And grow one in the sense of this world's life;
   And then, the low song
When the dead man is praised on his journey—
   'Bear, bear him along

'With his few faults shut up like dead flowrets;
   'Are balm-seeds not here
'To console us? The land has got none such
   'As he on the bier—
'Oh, would we might keep thee, my brother!'
   And then, the glad chaunt
Of the marriage,—first go the young maidens—
   Next, she whom we vaunt
As the beauty, the pride of our dwelling:
   And then, the great march
When man runs to man to assist him
   And buttress an arch
Nought can break ... who shall harm them, our brothers?
   Then, the chorus intoned
As the Levites go up to the altar
   In glory enthroned—
But I stopped here—for here, in the darkness,
   Saul groaned.

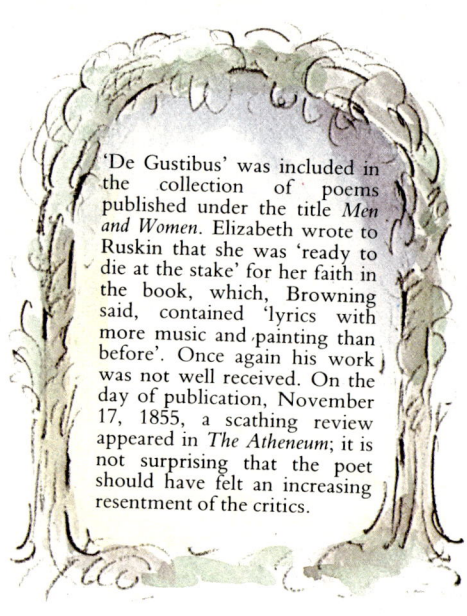

'De Gustibus' was included in the collection of poems published under the title *Men and Women*. Elizabeth wrote to Ruskin that she was 'ready to die at the stake' for her faith in the book, which, Browning said, contained 'lyrics with more music and painting than before'. Once again his work was not well received. On the day of publication, November 17, 1855, a scathing review appeared in *The Atheneum*; it is not surprising that the poet should have felt an increasing resentment of the critics.

## 'De Gustibus—'

YOUR ghost will walk, you lover of trees,
  (If our loves remain)
    In an English lane,
By a cornfield-side a-flutter with poppies.
Hark, those two in the hazel coppice—
A boy and a girl, if the good fates please,
  Making love, say,—
    The happier they!
Draw yourself up from the light of the moon,
And let them pass, as they will too soon,
  With the beanflowers' boon,
    And the blackbird's tune,
    And May, and June!

What I love best in all the world
Is a castle, precipice-encurled,
In a gash of the wind-grieved Apennine.
Or look for me, old fellow of mine,
(If I get my head from out the mouth
O' the grave, and loose my spirit's bands,
And come again to the land of lands)—
In a sea-side house to the farther South,
Where the baked cicala die of drouth,
And one sharp tree—'tis a cypress—stands,
By the many hundred years red-rusted,
Rough iron-spiked, ripe fruit-o'ercrusted,
My sentinel to guard the sands
To the water's edge. For, what expands
Before the house, but the great opaque
Blue breadth of sea without a break?
While, in the house, for ever crumbles

Some fragment of the frescoed walls,
From blisters where a scorpion sprawls.
A girl bare-footed brings, and tumbles
Down on the pavement, green-flesh melons,
And says there's news to-day—the king
Was shot at, touched in the liver-wing,
Goes with his Bourbon arm in a sling:
—She hopes they have not caught the felons.
Italy, my Italy!
Queen Mary's saying serves for me—
   (When fortune's malice
   Lost her—Calais)—
Open my heart and you will see
Graved inside of it, 'Italy.'
Such lovers old are I and she:
So it always was, so shall ever be!

First published in 1845, this lyric in praise of spring-time in England must rank as one of the best-loved poems in the English language. Its power to conjure up so succinctly the paradise of the countryside in April and May has made it a favourite that stands the test of time.

## Home Thoughts, From Abroad

OH, to be in England
Now that April's there,
And whoever wakes in England
Sees, some morning, unaware,
That the lowest boughs and the brushwood sheaf
Round the elm-tree bole are in tiny leaf,
While the chaffinch sings on the orchard bough
In England—now!

And after April, when May follows,
And the whitethroat builds, and all the swallows!
Hark, where my blossomed pear-tree in the hedge
Leans to the field and scatters on the clover
Blossoms and dewdrops—at the bent spray's edge—
That's the wise thrush; he sings each song twice over,
Lest you should think he never could recapture
The first fine careless rapture!
And though the fields look rough with hoary dew
All will be gay when noontide wakes anew
The buttercups, the little children's dower
—Far brighter than this gaudy melon-flower!

'Robert and I have had a very happy Winter in Florence,' wrote Elizabeth in March, 1853. She had at last begun her most famous work 'Aurora Leigh' while her husband was working on the poems which were to make up the volumes *Men and Women* published in 1855. 'Their Last Ride Together' was included in this publication and is considered by his critics to be one of the best of Browning's love poems.

## The Last Ride

I SAID—Then, dearest, since 't is so,
Since now at length my fate I know,
Since nothing all my love avails,
Since all, my life seemed meant for, fails,
    Since this was written and needs must be—
My whole heart rises up to bless
Your name in pride and thankfulness!
Take back the hope you gave,—I claim
Only a memory of the same,
—And this beside, if you will not blame,
    Your leave for one more last ride with me.

My mistress bent that brow of hers;
Those deep dark eyes where pride demurs
When pity would be softening through,
Fixed me a breathing-while or two
    With life or death in the balance: right!
The blood replenished me again;
My last thought was at least not vain:
I and my mistress, side by side
Shall be together, breathe and ride,
So, one day more am I deified.
    Who knows but the world may end to-night?

Hush! if you saw some western cloud
All billowy-bosomed, over-bowed
By many benedictions—sun's
And moon's and evening-star's at once—
   And so, you, looking and loving best,
Conscious grew, your passion drew
Cloud, sunset, moonrise, star-shine too,
Down on you, near and yet more near,
Till flesh must fade for heaven was here!—
Thus leant she and lingered—joy and fear!
   Thus lay she a moment on my breast.

Then we began to ride. My soul
Smoothed itself out, a long-cramped scroll
Freshening and fluttering in the wind.
Past hopes already lay behind.
   What need to strive with a life awry?
Had I said that, had I done this,
So might I gain, so might I miss.
Might she have loved me? just as well
She might have hated, who can tell!
Where had I been now if the worst befell?
   And here we are riding, she and I.

Who knows what's fit for us? Had fate
Proposed bliss here should sublimate
My being—had I signed the bond—
Still one must lead some life beyond,
   Have a bliss to die with, dim-descried.
This foot once planted on the goal,
This glory-garland round my soul,
Could I descry such? Try and test!
I sink back shuddering from the quest.
Earth being so good, would heaven seem best?
   Now, heaven and she are beyond this ride.

And yet—she has not spoke so long!
What if heaven be that, fair and strong
At life's best, with our eyes upturned
Whither life's flower is first discerned,
   We, fixed so, ever should so abide?
What if we still ride on, we two
With life for ever old yet new,
Changed not in kind but in degree
The instant made eternity,—
And heaven just prove that I and she
   Ride, ride together, for ever ride?

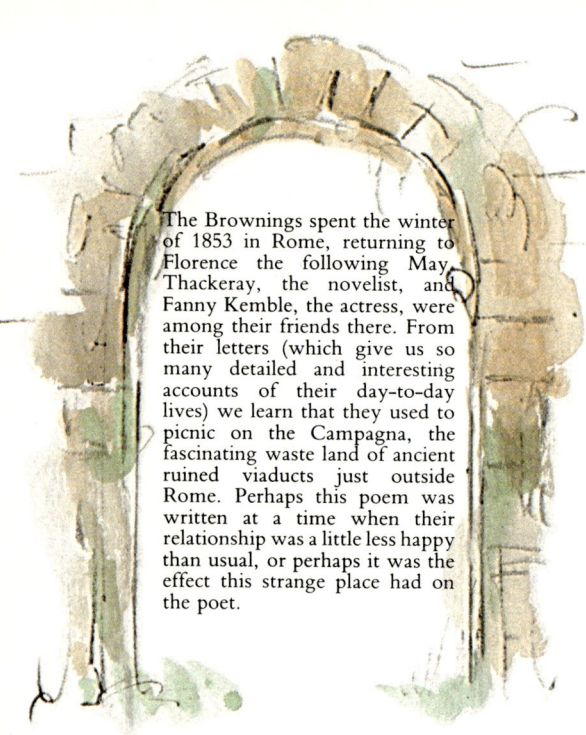

The Brownings spent the winter of 1853 in Rome, returning to Florence the following May. Thackeray, the novelist, and Fanny Kemble, the actress, were among their friends there. From their letters (which give us so many detailed and interesting accounts of their day-to-day lives) we learn that they used to picnic on the Campagna, the fascinating waste land of ancient ruined viaducts just outside Rome. Perhaps this poem was written at a time when their relationship was a little less happy than usual, or perhaps it was the effect this strange place had on the poet.

## Two in the Campagna

I WONDER do you feel to-day
    As I have felt since, hand in hand,
We sat down on the grass, to stray
    In spirit better through the land,
This morn of Rome and May?

For me, I touched a thought, I know,
    Has tantalized me many times,
(Like turns of thread the spiders throw
    Mocking across our path) for rhymes
To catch at and let go.

Help me to hold it! First it left
    The yellowing fennel, run to seed
There, branching from the brickwork's cleft,
    Some old tomb's ruin: yonder weed
Took up the floating weft,

Where one small orange cup amassed
    Five beetles,—blind and green they grope
Among the honey-meal: and last,
    Everywhere on the grassy slope
I traced it. Hold it fast!

The champaign with its endless fleece
  Of feathery grasses everywhere!
Silence and passion, joy and peace,
  An everlasting wash of air—
Rome's ghost since her decease.

Such life here, through such lengths of hours,
  Such miracles performed in play,
Such primal naked forms of flowers,
  Such letting nature have her way
While heaven looks from its towers!

How say you? Let us, O my dove,
  Let us be unashamed of soul,
As earth lies bare to heaven above!
  How is it under our control
To love or not to love?

I would that you were all to me,
  You that are just so much, no more.
Nor yours nor mine, nor slave nor free!
  Where does the fault lie? What the core
O' the wound, since wound must be?

I would I could adopt your will,
   See with your eyes, and set my heart
Beating by yours, and drink my fill
   At your soul's springs,—your part my part
In life, for good and ill.

No. I yearn upward, touch you close,
   Then stand away. I kiss your cheek,
Catch your soul's warmth,—I pluck the rose
   And love it more than tongue can speak—
Then the good minute goes.

Already how am I so far
   Out of that minute? Must I go
Still like the thistle-ball, no bar,
   Onward, whenever light winds blow,
Fixed by no friendly star?

Just when I seemed about to learn!
   Where is the thread now? Off again!
The old trick! Only I discern—
   Infinite passion, and the pain
Of finite hearts that yearn.

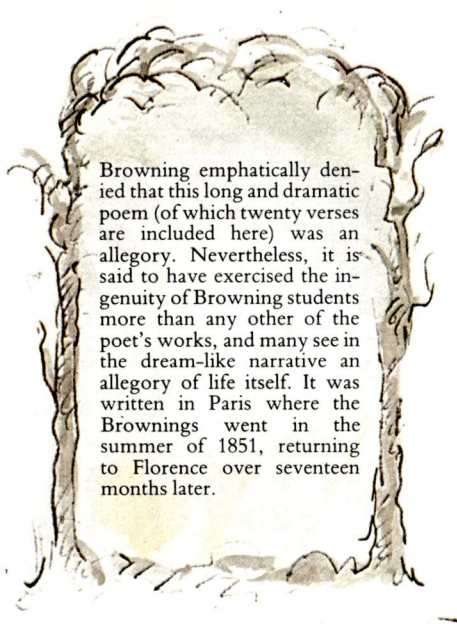

Browning emphatically denied that this long and dramatic poem (of which twenty verses are included here) was an allegory. Nevertheless, it is said to have exercised the ingenuity of Browning students more than any other of the poet's works, and many see in the dream-like narrative an allegory of life itself. It was written in Paris where the Brownings went in the summer of 1851, returning to Florence over seventeen months later.

## 'Childe Roland to the Dark Tower Came'

My first thought was, he lied in every word,
  That hoary cripple, with malicious eye
  Askance to watch the working of his lie
On mine, and mouth scarce able to afford
Suppression of the glee, that pursed and scored
  Its edge, at one more victim gained thereby.

What else should he be set for, with his staff?
  What, save to waylay with his lies, ensnare
  All travellers who might find him posted there,
And ask the road? I guessed what skull-like laugh
Would break, what crutch 'gin write my epitaph
  For pastime in the dusty thoroughfare,

If at his counsel I should turn aside
  Into that ominous tract which, all agree,
  Hides the Dark Tower. Yet acquiescingly
I did turn as he pointed; neither pride
Nor hope rekindling at the end descried,
  So much as gladness that some end might be.

Thus, I had so long suffered in this quest,
  Heard failure prophesied so oft, been writ
  So many times among 'The Band'—to wit,
The knights who to the Dark Tower's search addressed
Their steps—that just to fail as they, seemed best,
  And all the doubt was now—should I be fit?

So, quiet as despair, I turned from him,
  That hateful cripple, out of his highway
  Into the path he pointed. All the day
Had been a dreary one at best, and dim
Was settling to its close, yet shot one grim
  Red leer to see the plain catch its estray.

For mark! no sooner was I fairly found
  Pledged to the plain, after a pace or two,
  Than, pausing to throw backward a last view
O'er the safe road, 't was gone; grey plain all round:
Nothing but plain to the horizon's bound.
  I might go on; nought else remained to do.

So, on I went. I think I never saw
  Such starved ignoble nature; nothing throve:
  For flowers—as well expect a cedar grove!
But cockle, spurge, according to their law
Might propagate their kind, with none to awe,
  You'd think; a burr had been a treasure-trove.

No! penury, inertness and grimace,
   In some strange sort, were the land's portion. 'See
   Or shut your eyes,' said Nature peevishly,
'It nothing skills: I cannot help my case:
''T is the Last Judgment's fire must cure this place,
   'Calcine its clods and set my prisoners free.'

If there pushed any ragged thistle-stalk
   Above its mates, the head was chopped; the bents
   Were jealous else. What made those holes and rents
In the dock's harsh swarth leaves, bruised as to baulk
All hope of greenness? 't is a brute must walk
   Pashing their life out, with a brute's intents.

As for the grass, it grew as scant as hair
   In leprosy, thin dry blades pricked the mud
   Which underneath looked kneaded up with blood.
One stiff blind horse, his every bone a-stare,
Stood stupefied, however he came there:
   Thrust out past service from the devil's stud!

Alive? he might be dead for aught I know,
   With that red gaunt and colloped neck a-strain,
   And shut eyes underneath the rusty mane;
Seldom went such grotesqueness with such woe;
I never saw a brute I hated so;
   He must be wicked to deserve such pain.

And just as far as ever from the end!
   Nought in the distance but the evening, nought
   To point my footstep further! At the thought,
A great black bird, Apollyon's bosom-friend,
Sailed past, nor beat his wide wing dragon-penned
   That brushed my cap—perchance the guide I sought.

For, looking up, aware I somehow grew,
   'Spite of the dusk, the plain had given place
   All round to mountains—with such name to grace
Mere ugly heights and heaps now stolen in view.
How thus they had surprised me,—solve it, you!
   How to get from them was no clearer case.

Yet half I seemed to recognize some trick
   Of mischief happened to me, God knows when—
   In a bad dream perhaps. Here ended, then,
Progress this way. When, in the very nick
Of giving up, one time more, came a click
   As when a trap shuts—you're inside the den!

Burningly it came on me all at once,
   This was the place! those two hills on the right,
   Crouched like two bulls locked horn in horn in fight;
While to the left, a tall scalped mountain ... Dunce,
Dotard, a-dozing at the very nonce,
   After a life spent training for the sight!

What in the midst lay but the Tower itself?
   The round squat turret, blind as the fool's heart,
   Built of brown stone, without a counterpart
In the whole world. The tempest's mocking elf
Points to the shipman thus the unseen shelf
   He strikes on, only when the timbers start.

Not see? because of night perhaps?—why, day
   Came back again for that! before it left,
   The dying sunset kindled through a cleft:
The hills, like giants at a hunting, lay,
Chin upon hand, to see the game at bay,—
   'Now stab and end the creature—to the heft!'

Not hear? when noise was everywhere! it tolled
   Increasing like a bell. Names in my ears
   Of all the lost adventurers my peers,—
How such a one was strong, and such was bold,
And such was fortunate, yet each of old
   Lost, lost! one moment knelled the woe of years.

There they stood, ranged along the hill-sides, met
   To view the last of me, a living frame
   For one more picture! in a sheet of flame
I saw them and I knew them all. And yet
Dauntless the slug-horn to my lips I set,
   And blew. '*Childe Roland to the Dark Tower came.*'

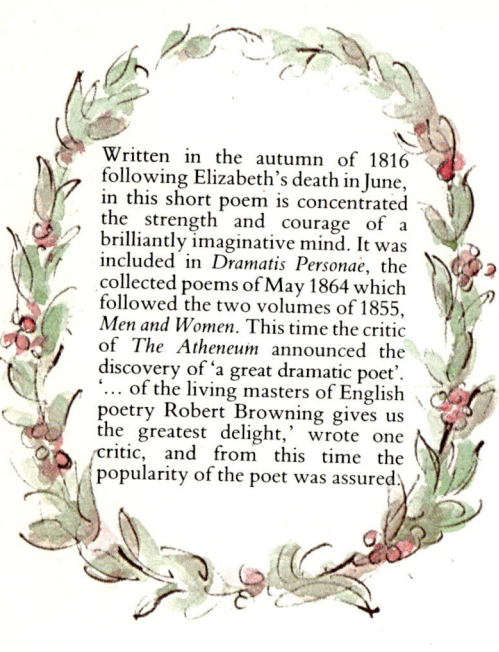

Written in the autumn of 1816 following Elizabeth's death in June, in this short poem is concentrated the strength and courage of a brilliantly imaginative mind. It was included in *Dramatis Personae*, the collected poems of May 1864 which followed the two volumes of 1855, *Men and Women*. This time the critic of *The Atheneum* announced the discovery of 'a great dramatic poet'. '... of the living masters of English poetry Robert Browning gives us the greatest delight,' wrote one critic, and from this time the popularity of the poet was assured.

## Prospice

FEAR death?—to feel the fog in my throat,
    The mist in my face,
When the snows begin, and the blasts denote
    I am nearing the place,
The power of the night, the press of the storm,
    The post of the foe;
Where he stands, the Arch Fear in a visible form,
    Yet the strong man must go:
For the journey is done and the summit attained,
    And the barriers fall,
Though a battle's to fight ere the guerdon be gained,
    The reward of it all.
I was ever a fighter, so—one fight more,
    The best and the last!
I would hate that death bandaged my eyes, and forbore,
    And bade me creep past.
No! let me taste the whole of it, fare like my peers
    The heroes of old,
Bear the brunt, in a minute pay glad life's arrears
    Of pain, darkness and cold.
For sudden the worst turns the best to the brave,
    The black minute's at end,
And the elements' rage, the fiend-voices that rave,
    Shall dwindle, shall blend,
Shall change, shall become first a peace out of pain,
    Then a light, then thy breast,
O thou soul of my soul! I shall clasp thee again,
    And with God be the rest!